FANATIC
HEART

Books by Deborah Pope

A Separate Vision
Fanatic Heart
Mortal World
Falling Out of the Sky
Take Nothing

FANATIC HEART

Deborah Pope

Carnegie Mellon University Press
Pittsburgh 2022

Cover design by Connie Amoroso

Library of Congress Control Number: 2021947333
ISBN: 978-0-88748-679-1
Copyright © 1992 by Deborah Pope
Printed and bound in the United States of America

10 9 8 7 6 5 4 3 2 1

Fanatic Heart was first published by Louisiana State University Press,
Baton Rouge, Louisiana, in 1992.

First Carnegie Mellon University Press Classic Contemporaries Edition,
February 2022

Some of these poems first appeared in the following periodicals, sometimes in slightly
different form: *And Review*, "Passage"; *Archive*, "Rousseau, *Les Joueurs*, 1908" and
"On the Mountain"; *CutBank*, "Rape"; *Madison Review*, "Patrick's Point"; *New Laurel
Review*, "The Boy on Roan Mountain" and "Frank Benson, *Portrait of My Daughters*,
1907"; *Ohio Review*, "There Is Something"; *Poem*, "Preparation"; *Poetry Miscellany*,
"Palmer Lake"; *Poetry Northwest*, "Happy"; *Southern Poetry Review*, "What
We Meant to Say," "The Dentist," and "Firstborn"; *Southern Review*, "Equinox";
and *Tar River Poetry*, "Another Valentine."

"Peaches" first appeared in *Cardinal: A Contemporary Anthology
of Fiction and Poetry by North Carolina Writers*, ed. Richard Krawiec
(Wendell, N.C.: Jacar Press, 1986).

for Dean

Contents

I

Passage

The emptying moon tips
just above the treeline.
We are the only car on the road.
So dark the night, so close
the line of trees,
it is as if we had gone

under the earth, or the ill-
colored wick of moon was
the lantern astern on a ship
that had cut us adrift.
We move in another dimension.
Moths swim up in our headlights

like ghost fish darting
in black water. The silence
of acceptance or calamity
seeps through the glass.
Already your knuckles
look like coral on the wheel.

The children sleep in shapes
they will settle to in time
on the ocean floor, their bones
uncollected, like a necklace
broken in the sand.
What did any of it come to?

The only light is what
we carry with us.
There is salt in my kiss.

Another Valentine

I have come to expect
forsythia stunning
the ragged twigs with random yellow,
the hard spears forking
from the rat's nest of February.
I have come to expect
the south wind treading the lawn
while snow still heaps
like egg shells
in the shade.

Moving up stairs all afternoon
the four o'clock light
holes up in our room,
fingers the careless sheets.
The closets are holding their breath.
In the kitchen stiff cuttings
clatter in a glass jar,
pink clots of quince.
I have had the clippers waiting.

And you, you
sweat easily all morning
raking the winter away,
come in with cool edges,
the smell of raw sun
in your palms,
swing open my heart like a hinge.
I have come to expect it.

Salter Path

I

I came here looking for my life.
I cannot find it in all this blank.
I want to look longer,
but your work, it is impossible.
I have work. It is impossible.
I say to you, save me.
You look kind, change the subject,
hold me when I do not want it.
All week the children grow bold,
but for us, they would run
into the water and never stop,
so light, they barely print the sand.
It sifts through all our rooms,
chafes my dreams.

II

Light peels low and ragged
in the east, where I walk
the moon has not yet set.
My youngest would not come with me.
Last chance, I told him, suit yourself.
Out of habit I am looking
for something to carry back,
carapaces, bones, tokens
of apology. Shells are few,
and broken, unlike the whole
perfect forms there once were
when I came with my friend
before I married.
Pushing in the wind we found all
we could hold, cupped, intact,
the surprising, delicate
undersides pink and raw
as our bodies.

III

Passing shuttered cottages,
diminishing dunes, ever wider
sweeps of space,
I do not want to go on.
The ocean empties each effort
to think, the monotony
of its crude maneuver,
its stupid return and spill.
The waves heave up like gelatin,
smooth, translucent,
but it is common and dull
to say so. Better to say
they are marble, cold,
emerald marble,
as they hurl and arc,
hurl and arc, rip
their white hearts
from the center, out.

Two A.M.

I lie folded as if for burial,
your sleeping, stuttering gutterals
wheezing like an engine
that won't turn over.
Some large nocturnal animal
is chuck-chucking on the porch,
and a skitter sloops the roof
like squirrels or first rain.
I listen to the tinker of dark,
the creak I hear as wind
and not wind, think of women
bloodied in their beds,
nipples sliced, the head
on a shelf, there may be tapes,
the authorities won't say,
they say this beats all.
Whenever I dream this, this is
true, whenever I think this,
this is happening.
To hear the lock lift would
be what I had always expected.
I long for rain,
I long for my child to cry out,
but he goes on as only
he can with the steady
small bellows of his belly,
his sleep soured head
in the crook of his arm.

Planting in December

I don't know why I'm doing it,
hunched over out here,
every part of me pulled
against winds, bearing down
on the trowel,
its handle gutting
my red palms deeper
than its spooned steel
in the dirt.

The bulbs loll like doll
heads in their plastic mesh,
creamy and featureless
as soft-serve, the same minarets,
tiny buds like tongues
at their tips. I am doing it
too late, holes too shallow,
the red clay clumping
over something like caramel.

I shove each deep as I can,
thump the earth flat
with palm and boot,
no different from burial.
The stiff afternoon is a fist
pushing me, clumsy with cold.
Forgive me,
it is like so much I do.
I breathe on my knuckles,
reach deeper, bend sharper.

Signs

The real constitution of each thing
is accustomed to hide itself.
—Heraclitus

I

Our house blurs into this winter rain,
the contours of our land emerge
in watersheds and shadow.
A grounding returns to the sense of things.
Last night we saw a great barred owl
on the topmost limb of ironwood,
fixed as a boundary stone
on some old, high road.
For a moment it was remarkable,
then simply part of what was there.
We stood at the center of a compass
of trees, such clarity in each degree,
brilliant dusk receding all around,
the middle decade of a life
gone with it.

II

Morning light haloes our children,
tips of twigs suspend
fine seed pearls of rain.
Our fingers lace a momentary tent.
In these woods we have chosen
with scarcely more knowing
than we chose each other,
prospects will always promise
more than they come to.
The solidity of this house is surface,
the permanence of anything is myth.
We take our visions edged,
at home in a light that curves.
Still, as the gypsies say,
good road.

III

I pride myself as one too wise
for wishes, too wry to read
loose portents in these pines,
yet something in me longs
this day to wish you, on the chance,
such fragile talismans prove true,
that you may know whole years
as single as our children's faces,
light you carry with you
like these leaves,
and have the sight that finds
in vagrant rivulets of rain
maps that make a difference
in the way you live.

The Boy on Roan Mountain

For days he wandered in that wilderness
until all green looked the same,
afraid of raccoon and catamount,
afraid of the dark closet at home.
Two hundred searchers began,
at the end only a handful hung on.
They will seek him in dreams,
volunteers growing old,
but the boy will be eight forever,
fearful of fists, confused by rain,
the cold that crept up
the switchbacks two days on.

He was sighted here and there
by isolated folk, heard calling,
Daddy, I'm coming out,
but he never emerged from the laurel and pine
where the mountain drew him in.
Wherever he wandered, coatless and pale,
no one followed, whatever trunk
he leaned on to wait, its shadow
fell on no trail his mother knew.
His BBs turned to stones in the stream,
the sky was no blanker than a ceiling.
Did he know what love called
through the bullhorns and mists,
did it close on the twig-thin arm,
as he cut where the brush was unbent,
miles from the last, lost road,
where rescue and escape alike
are the final dreams of children.

Photograph of a Woman Homesteader, Montana, 1870

There are no bars more pitiless
than this blankness, the endless
sweep of buffalo grass as far
as the incongruous camera reaches.
She is wearing her best, a collar
hand-stitched to a style she knew
in Ohio, or Missouri, the girlish hat
carried in her lap a thousand miles
in a wagon that wouldn't take
another ax or bit.
She stands amidst the plain
as someone posed before a scene
rolled in behind her.
Only the hands are right,
stiff in the heavy, hide gloves.

If she has gone mad from famine
or blizzard, insects or prairie fire,
delivering herself over and over,
cords cut, a child lost, days
before the doctor came, going
months without hearing her nearest
neighbor, thinking nothing is so loud
as this hush, what of that.
There is something fanatic
in every heart. The direction
she has come from is gone.

Ritual

The days go on
and nothing happens.
We talk of leaving,
together or apart.
Under the surgery
of February, our street
looks gritty and urban.
A bleach bottle cracks
in a gash of snow,
Tonkas up-end
in another dead shrub.
No matter what we stick
in that ragged dirt
between brick and cement
each spring it's carted out
brittle and stiff.
Last year a camellia
foolhardy with buds
in icy rain like today
got lopped for its trouble.

A third-hand Buick sits
at the curb,
our good car is older
than the kids combined.
They ride their trikes
where they can,
six feet and turn,
six feet and turn,
imagining where they're not.
My knuckles are splitting
out here, gusts of traffic
whipping as they pass.
Cold pushes like thumbs

in my ears,
but I can hold out
longer against it.
The air is sharp,
but not sharp enough.

Sorrowing

Tonight I run the bath for my son,
holding his small, white body
in my hands, pouring water
over his seaweed hair,
his thin limbs like slippery fish.
I am thinking of you,
your unspeakable grief,
how every act I do,
these simplest of motions
of mother and child and water,
were done by you
for your child,
how forever you will stroke
and touch her, know
in your hands the shape
of the place she has been,
cup water for her dreaming head,
your daughter,
your child,
who is dead.

Outside a drumming rain goes on,
cold, rising,
your pain kindles
everything I touch,
cloth, comb, cup,
it was never to be like this.
Over and over I wash the body
of my son, so new yet
from the waters of my own,
but already he is slipping
where I cannot reach or save.

On the Mountain

for Judith McDade

You would have been climbing all morning,
moving patiently, carefully,
over the sunlit rocks,
bending to the pitch of the slope,
breathing the pine,
feeling the cooling air.
Somewhere in those hours
you would have passed the timberline,
moving into the time
of the mountains, climbing closer
to the beginning, becoming
older with every reach.
If you had looked back
at the green camp
lying between two fingers of snow,
the small world you were leaving
must have seemed no more
than the moss at your feet,
the clouds at your hand,
when you turned
and stepped into the sky.

Even in death you are more vivid
than any of us, more vivid than this day,
a high, deep cloudless blue,
the full light of late October,
the autumn-turning trees.
All over the ground, numberless,
lie fallen ginkgo leaves,
bright as stones underwater,
lovely, yellow ginkgo leaves
pooling the shade,
the color of your wind-scattered hair.
Nothing I know answers for this.

What We Meant to Say

If we could go one afternoon
when chicory turned the blue
of the sky, goldenrod burned
in the fields, and the dust
lay flat on the road,
I would tell you what
you could not tell me
that autumn night you held me
hard against the car
in the darkest corner
of the lot, saying,
give it to me, give it to me.
You could not say,
years will come when
you know how little I ask,
how little this means,
life does not shake
for such trifles.
I tell you, he will never
see your loveliness
who is himself still lovely.
He will never know how
your hands ache, your mouth,
you want it. No one
is watching, they are only
peering into the night
outside the windows.
Isn't it obvious?
Tomorrow you will hold your face
from the light, hide
your thighs in the sheets.

It is not love, but lack
of imagination binds you.

Listen, there come times
you must act without thought
of anything more than time,
when there can be no fidelity
to anything more than a moment
when everything is right,
the set you've been waiting for,
sky, fields, moon like a marquee,
when nothing else matters
but what you will risk,
what your mouth will open upon.
There are boys so beautiful
they hurt your eyes,
fingers so strange
on your skin your body
was never yours before,
voices in the dark whose words
come new on your tongue.
Nothing waits, nothing comes back.
Every moment that ever mattered
to me has not happened.
Lean down,
life is running like a sieve.

II

Hard Climb Road

for my grandmother

I

Driving home to her funeral in September,
we head down the Piedmont,
taking the freeways that run by fields
and outlet malls, morning stretching away
under the benign and vacant blue skies
Carolina is known for.
A Greensboro station plays oldies in the car,
and loss only lasts till the next dance.
Outside Mt. Airy, we pick up two lanes
through Cana, Galax, and Fancy Gap,
past the hillbilly markets and stands,
molasses, apples, and Dixie kitsch,
trailing pony-tailed girls in pickups.
The day is cool and clear, a weekend
to dream, or retrieve, of family rides
in fall, a peaceful film unfolding
of southeastern hills and farms,
silos and satellite dishes,
sheep still as stones in the fields.
In Virginia, the new road's half done,
shale shingling up where the cut is rawest.
My sons sing out at every crane,
thrill through blasting zones.
We fly down the far side of vistas
that make majesty almost tangible,
forests like a murky pool we sink in,
greening as we surface.

II

We enter the earth at Big Walker Tunnel,
come out to the random Calvary crosses
driven in by guerrilla believers
on the steep slopes of West Virginia.
Near Bluefield, the "Gospel Light Trio"

goes by in a bus. Now the pines rise
straight from the interstate,
the turnpike traversing rock risers
high over towns named Paint Creek,
Cabin Creek, Skitter, and Laurel.
Hollow into hollow, valleys interlock
their fingers, our road winding
like a rosary between them.
By late afternoon, we are skirting Charleston.
The children pester and fight,
sleep and stare, their hours dragging.
They know nothing of the passage
that has called us back.
So young, they forget even this
as it happens, will hardly remember
a figure so spectral and frail.
I remember holding old prints of her
in furs and leghorn hat, laughter
rare for photographs of those days,
the backdrops a lawn lunch
or running board, beaux with beards
and pocket swags. She said to me once,
I do not feel old, it is only
something about my face.
In the dusk beyond the window,
I imagine her last meal of chocolate
and broth spooned in by my father,
her head like a boiled egg under his hand.

        III
Outside St. Albans, we take 35 North.
The crossroads of Winfield,
Fenton, Frazier's Bottom,
drowse on the Ohio floodplain.
This is a sky that knows limits,
even the animals are few enough to point at,
Angus like burned stumps in the fields.
Voting signs fly by, lifted in the wind
that stirs the weeds in unhitched harrows,
petunias in painted tires.
At Morgan's Landing, in their giant alembics,

the nukes bubble and brew.
There is an air as if the people had gone,
left work waiting in the yard,
the tobacco half-strung, gone in
from the baskets and clotheslines,
where shirts flap brainlessly,
like hands endlessly waving goodbye.

IV

When we come to the river at Gallipolis,
we are on the last leg home.
We have crossed four states
to reach the dark, the sky
like an afterglow of great conflagration.
Clouds move in a long, slow barge.
In the quiet universe of the car
the children sleep.
Lights of the cars ahead burn like coals.
All seems suspended in time.
The names of county roads fall away
in our headlights—Grace's Run,
Tranquility Pike, Hard Climb Road—
they toll the stations as we pass.
We are almost home.
Along the ridge the twilight trees
move like a procession
of women in black mantillas
bearing the moon aloft,
the delicate tracery of
their silhouettes vanishing.
At last, it rises free,
a piece of ivory,
a bright bone,
a slip of a thing,
washed smooth and clean
in the long pull of the dark.

Palmer Lake

We stayed in cabins we were hardly
ever in, lived on docks, corn on the cob,
all morning we hung over piers,
dove from floats, clanked on drums
where weeds lifted like green beards.
Mothers sat through hot noons
in bright, metal chairs shaped like
dippers we traced in the skies at night,
fathers built bamboo poles,
peed from boats, and taught us
"True Blue Bill" over evening dishes.
At dusk we chased semaphores of fireflies
until our names just faintly reached us
from pools of yellow light,
where fathers played cards
and grandfathers idly searched
for crawlers in the shadows.
Bedtimes were brief calms
that luffed into mists, wet grass,
the cold grip of gunnels, slipping
off through gray silk, silent
over shallows rinsed with gold,
where childhood drifted,
and disappeared, with the dreaming,
casual symmetry of minnows.

Loose Ends

I

There are times I've never spoken of
to Mother or Penny, though surely
they remember better, and still,
for instance, that winter night
when you were packing,
carrying your shirts from hanger to bag,
your back to me in the high closet light.
I can see that dense sanctuary
of hatboxes and ties,
hear your buckles on the door.
I was sitting on the bed
in my Brownie uniform,
a beanie still on my head,
you were wearing your office whites,
a Kangol cap you had just put on
or never taken off.
You were crying.
I knew without asking
I could not go with you.
I did not know enough to be afraid.
I accepted it as absolutely
as anything else in childhood.

II

Up to this reel,
I have been yours.
I love your smoky, sour kiss
when late from parties
you tuck me in,
sometimes in your underwear
or just from returning the sitter,
the sharp cold in your coat
alive on my face.

I go now to the basement,
bring back a doll, tell you
this is to remember me by.
I am trying to do whatever it is
that must be expected of me,
then sit with Mother
in the sleeves of her robe
at the top of the stairs
watching you go.

III

Then simply, you are back,
after days or weeks.
I am good now at reading,
make up stories for friends,
whisper the word *intoxicated*
like magic stolen
from a giant's box.
I go to camp in summers,
lose your thick-wristed watch at school,
forget your receptionists' names.
One night in the kitchen
you come home from work,
slump on a stool.
I am setting the table,
getting the knives.
You flip through the mail,
see where your orthodontist friend
has had a fourth son,
say, some people
have all the luck.

The Dentist

I think of my father, all his life,
more with strangers than with us,
the years of his boast and wit
expended in the service of people
whose names we hardly knew,
his best lines delivered to an audience
of open mouths, rigid in the grimace
of permanent dental hilarity.
Nights at his lab bench, he bent
with watchmaker hands, jeweler's glass
to the blue Bunsen flame, clever
with pincers and pliers, dripping
the indigo wax on inlay casts,
carving, polishing, the scratchy
basement stereo sending out Sinatra
and Dorsey from the army issue,
metal-heavy discs of Korea,
or baseball crackling on hot, summer
evenings from the plastic Zenith
over the high, intermittent whistle
of drill. All those nights
he was down there, flecks of plaster
on his glasses, tobacco littering
the bright square of light,
while upstairs we went on with
our algebra, telephones, and piano,
winning and losing loves, growing up
and leaving. It is only lately
that I have begun to wonder what
he wanted, what he thought, hunched
over carver and pick, night after
night, placing one perfect, gold
molar gleaming in the fossil jaw.

Inheritance

She rakes me with failures,
with what she could say
if she wanted,
with all she has had to do
sorting the things of the dead
and not even her own—
their cut beads, lustreware,
saved stamps, and plate—
while father chimes in
it's all mine now anyhow,
I can do what I want,
and I flee
to the basement,
a husband on a fold-out couch,
incant, she can't
get me here,
though she follows
to the stairwell,
shrieking my name,
come up, we'll start over.
When I lift the phone
she is ringing my sisters
against me, and I shiver
in your shoulder,
don't make me go up,
oh, how can you love me,
pleading, let us leave now,
tonight, clean, forever,
yes, forever,
I am capable of that.

There Is Something

There is something of every good-bye in this.
Somehow it is always winter,
there is snow at the curb,
the driveways are gray,
The soles of your shoes
are turning dark and wet.
She stands there in her bathrobe.
She has just come from
packing sandwiches.
You are pushed by some schedule,
and the weather,
compelled by her voice,
which is speaking.
She kisses your cheek
and hands you your life
in the neat paper bag
For this moment in her face
all your seams are mended,
your habits white.
You hug her and smile.
Your gift is your silence,
you leave.
Yet later when you remember
it will be that always
her eyes were sad,
her hand on your sleeve.

Changeable Geography

The middle of May and speedwell
spindles in my garden
beside poppies, pinks,
new iris pointed and furled
as crayons, late tulips
like cinched umbrellas.
Over them, the goose-necked
columbines rise like spiny
sea life or satellites,
as if they could go far and deep.
I think of my mother's garden,
that stretch of dirt
behind our house in Ohio,
back where the rusted swingset
and picnic table sat.
Each spring she'd win it back
from brush and weed,
dig lilies, peonies,
a season's greens.
We picked white stalks
of wild phlox along its edge,
buried our dog in the corner
where it dipped below Slagle's garage,
and no one knew the lot line.

Those years, on summer Sundays,
we'd roll the windows down,
head up the interstate,
let county roads carry us
past fields simple as a puzzle,
crossroads with storefronts for rent,
where my father, his ring
nicking time on the wheel,
talked idly of staying, doing

whatever he had always
wanted to do, and my mother,
her passenger gaze turned away,
named old flowers leaning
in dooryards no one else passed.
We knew the name of nothing,
but grew unaccountably as beans,
ran wild as cucumber vines,
and followed the creek far
out of sound of the bell
my mother rang to call us in.

I kneel in my own garden now,
at the edge of my labor
the earth goes to riot and weed.
A child runs in the grass
beyond call. I wonder how
my mother raised so many.
We miss much when we are young.
Events strike somewhere above us
like rumors of a distant war.
It may be best so. Who knows
what will scar, what heal.
Now the slightest turnings
send me back into the past,
that blankness nudging into
words, shapes, the changeable
geography of memory.
I hold it like a heavy flower
I long to carry home.

III

Firstborn

I

Early light, listening for his sounds,
the birds' waking blending
with his calls, sighs—
look! there are birds in the cradles,
there are babies in the trees!

II

Stunned by this passion,
is this how it is, then?
Small bundle in the morning sheets,
boy against my naked skin,
warm, sour knit
of bodies, milk, hair.
Does one have another
to keep from going under
in love for the first?
I want to stifle every cry,
be happy always,
know no pain or needing.

III

Into his first autumn,
first fire,
snailing out from his covers,
tentative, absorbed.
On the garden calendar
we turn the months
to bright green canes,
wine-veined chard,
rich bruise of eggplant.
He roots in his own season,
cayenne suit, cauliflower fist,
pale dangler,
succulent apple boy.

IV

His hands touch wonderingly
as two lovers
who have found each other
after many years.
His arms rise with unutterable delicacy,
learning the nuances of air.
His beauty dazes me.

V

Warm, gusty, prodigal light,
the last such day of fall.
Roses wither on, willow leaves
float in the dog's bowl.
Whoever said roses are youth?
Their petals are the cheeks of the old,
ruddy, thick pinks,
uneven golds,
wax on their lips.
What did I worry about before?

VI

The tendril head turns quick and true
on his bird body.
This morning in bed, he searches
to nurse again.
Our folding is fierce.

VII

One day he rises
in a child's body.
Just yesterday he came,
disassembled, a bag of boy parts.
Now, for a moment,
as if flipping channels,
or glancing down the hall,
I see a face slip by,
the phantom he beguiles
in the window glass.
His face at twenty? forty?
From our arms, from our gates,
he struggles to be free.

VIII

There are petals from the trees
in the wind today.
Dogwoods drift before the car
like snow or old wishes.
Crab apples, redbud, weeping cherry
scatter across the cedar mulch
of neat suburban borders.
Our arthritic dog was hunkering
by the flower beds
when I found her this morning,
shuddering and askew.
She has never forgiven us.

IX

Some days I want my mother,
wonder where I am living,
how to explain this street, this city.
Yet often I feel free in the house,
am in it whole days.
With its high rooms, back stairs,
it seems like something
I have always wanted.

X

Overnight, the azaleas have burst
heavily forth.
A tangle of leaf and bud
creeps over the dry stalks.
Here, an ancient gardenia bush,
in a sheltered place,
close against the bricks,
did not survive the winter.
It is touch and go
with gardenias in this zone.
Still, long before our coming,
someone had kept it alive,
someone who knew more
about such things.

The Secret

Two years, and our son half seems
a preposterous ruse whose mastermind
has dropped from sight, some stranger's heir
we've been given the secret care of,
thrust through the window, slipped
in the hasty bed with barely time
to get our stories straight.
We have played along, try not to call
attention to ourselves, blend
into the scenery as *mother, father.*

But when, his bright hair flying,
he runs without looking back
into the tangible rain of willows,
where sunlight spills like wet paint
in the leaves, and shouts of others
leap the ravine, we know there is
someplace else he belongs,
like the plane he watches
drone high and small
through the August afternoon.

So far, no one has come
to take him back.
He breathes in the air of the place,
the neighbors have been paid off.
At night his head bobs absently in sleep.
It is only we who remember it
otherwise, lying in the fitful dark,
listening as the skeptical wind
still sighs, *whose boy,*
whose boy?

The Goodmother Croons of Little Hansel

His head has the heft of pumpernickel,
he is as smooth and round,
the fine hairs soft as butter.
He wobbles on his bottom
as if balancing fruit,
currant eyes, cherry-meat mouth,
the juicy, plump apple-skin skin.
How his arms loll like kipfel,
I want to pinch small pieces off.
Like choicest marzipan his ears,
his nose a rosette from the baker's pouch.
I will sweet talk my custard stick
and lick his lips.

My clever confection, deadly dumpling,
what must it be like in a cake
of a house, meringues for mirrors,
a crone waiting under those sugar shingles
for children to ring her gumdrops?
I could gobble my little nougat in a minute.
Ah, the good *rote grütze*,
his toothiest penuche!
Nibble, nibble,
la, the poor woman,
we could share a heart between us.
He dreams in my arms broad as a platter.

Late

It was one of those days in November,
misplaced from another springtime,
when light filled all the broom-stiff bushes
and trees stretched out like elaborate
plans for trees. We took our sweaters off,
easy in our bodies. The air smelled
like fresh-turned earth,
and the ground was springy from rain.
Our son danced in my shirt
that reached past his knees,
wherever he went trailing leaves.
They rode in his girl's hair, aglow
like the last ropes of willow
high in the four o'clock sun.
Held still, he would have taken root,
his careless boots already half gone
to dirt. Over and over, I combed
the metal tines through tangles
of maple, poplar, and oak,
stroke upon stroke of sheer, purposeful
motion, until small hills sat far apart
like beaver mounds on a grassy lake.

Stripped to your t-shirt,
you split kindling by the garage,
the baby called from the swing.
I could hold you all in my eyes.
The sycamores reached up from the creek
with branches like the cool, white
impossibly perfect dowels of chalk
you imagined locked in the teacher's drawer.
Tonight, I will creep back out
when the sun has gone down,
break off a limb,

and write one hundred times
on the blank slate of the sky:
I promise to be happy,
I promise to be happy.

Preparation

The mushrooms at the sink
are a good batch,
large, firm,
the loose, black dirt
still on their
thick pale stems.

I hold them to the tap,
rubbing their round, firm
heads and stems
with wet forefinger
and thumb
in smooth, slow circles.
The warm water runs

over my motion,
they slice clean,
and their ripe belly
white flesh sends
up between my fingers
the rich, underground
smell of you.

Patrick's Point

We take the trail over the headlands,
below us the sea, our steps
slipping in the soft dust,
pulling us downward
until we take the last
at a race, chasing jaggedly
back and back from waves
coursing in where others have
burned the white fingers of trees.
Faces taut with cold, we spread
the sand, probe the rank
matted hair of kelp, polyp,
the smooth underflesh of shells,
feeling the pale, hard curl
of their slits for the sly
glimmer of agates.
Our tongues touch like fishes,
wind shakes us in its fist,
we cannot keep our footing,
lids turn up, float away,
and the sky bends back
begins to return, folding
over us like the black
seine of the earth.

Frank Benson, Portrait of My Daughters, 1907

They are three, like fates or graces,
in the sunlight of summer and youth.
They might have met in an orchard,
or by their mother's grave,
so do their eyes go past each other.
Two are already young women,
their ribbons sober and black,
Only the youngest wears hers white,
a lily someone has floated there.
The eldest holds a bowl of red blooms,
the middle one waits in her coat
for the journey she will begin.

Daughters, daughters,
their father's tints whisper, holding
a moment more the light, the long
pause of their century's spring.
Even then they had gone from his dream,
the eldest thrusting her fingers
deep in the bunched petals,
the middle one turning away,
and the youngest holding
her yet loose hair like a rope
she is poised to cut.

Klimt, The Fulfillment

In a night of brown stars, she undulates
against the kneeling trunk of his body.
He holds her at chin and temple,
his lips to the angle of her cheek,
pale under the breakwater of his bones.
His eyes hidden, he is telling her
how the egg shell of her face
feels in the grip of his fingers,
how the cerulean of forgotten skies
sighs in the hollow of her eyelids.
Planets orbit the folds of his robe,
its hem in golden vines that spangle
over the curve of her ankles.
Only the nimbus of his arms holds her
on the edge of green and violet time.
He is telling her this as her hand
reaches over, as if to pluck a string.
From his throat, heavy as a tree in fall,
she waits, unhurried, to hear
her one note sound.

Rousseau, Les Joueurs, *1908*

They leap formally in the tight clearing
like well-trained pugilists,
their joints surprising as marionettes.
Held in the stripes of bathers or convicts
they rise higher than the low limbs of trees,
whose trunks open like the mouths of birds,
whose leaves are thick as feathers.
Two men have turned the color of leaves,
red and gold, they are becoming smaller.
Eyes fixed above the clipped moustaches,
they cannot see their wood-cut hands
turning to claws. Beneath them,
the ground has been picked clean
of everything but the shadows of leaping.
In the sky, a giant beak moves
out of the tops of trees.
It is coming for the bright ball,
the blood-colored moon,
which is its eye.

Rape

No, I say,
don't lock the door,
I'll wait awhile—
and follow you outside.
Cradling the key, we watch you leave,
the dog and I, waving to
your turned head.
The evening settles and I fill
her red bowl with water
from the green hose curling
in the wet mint, the palest peach
blooms amid the nasturtiums
under the tap, the herbs near flowering.
People going home from the park
carry the sun down the street.
The dog runs after them
and summer birds beat
in the last rainpools.
Enveloping dusk comes up the steps.
Ahead of the dark, I enter
the house, lock the door.
In an ordinary yard,
in an ordinary time,
I am afraid
and you are afraid for me.
Another life
lifts its skirts over the grass,
dances away.

Still Life with Flowers

The scent of gardenias rides the evening air.
Late June, and their suffocating vanilla
fills my rooms, it is like a sickness,
I cannot get enough, carry the drooping
blooms inside to float in shallow dishes
until their odorous ivory turns.
They are whiter than babies' teeth,
draw me away from my son's smell,
his stiff, sour hair.
He will not sleep, blunders
at my side as I write.
What was that phrase?
Upstairs we rock in the heat
of his room, watch for storm light.
My husband calls reminding
to close the car windows.
In the waiting air the mimosas
seem already pressing their leaves
into articulate, fern fossils.
My son startles in dream.
Outside the midnight house
gardenias, lotus-like,
trail their rich pall
over the sill.

Happy

How prone we are to such flourishes,
the stagy fixings of time
in superlatives of ecstasy or pain—
that was the happiest day of his life,
that was the saddest she'd ever been,
I'll never forget that sight—
it is as if we needed these runes
to assure ourselves we did
in fact somewhere in our lives
feel the wingsweep of joy,
the fierce hug of grief,
once breathe in the unforgettable.

Were we not often happy
on ordinary days, when nothing
especially happened
to shimmer in memory's amber?
We only grade the days
we can remember at all,
and then for eccentric things,
the tipsy flower girl,
photographers delayed by snow,
the stripe in the funeral director's lapel.
What we really mean
is how unusual those moments were
from the customed round of living.
But it may have been
one's happiest day
was a usual day,
with nothing to pin it on,
a Wednesday, say,
or Sunday afternoon, perhaps in fall,
when the weather was nothing remarkable,
the children played a nameless game,

and the chair you were reading in
went years later in a curb sale.
Imagine long light came through scant leaves,
the lawn lingered on, unraked,
a stew simmered in the kitchen.
A dog, the color of autumn herself,
slept by the grate.
It was the year you knew
where your family was,
you could pick up a phone
and hear the voice
of everyone you cared for.

Yes, I remember it now.
You were there,
the sun just slipping
below the trees.

Peaches

Last night I dreamed I turned to you
from the low porch chair,
we were old,
but in your eyes I was still
the girl you followed
into another life,
hair long, feet small,
my back the exact span of your hand.

Tonight I will dream
I am in the yard perhaps,
bending stiffly in the garden, apron pinned,
amid the late beans and zinnias.
I will lift my head and see you
coming over the grass, and wish again
that I might see you always so,
moving towards me.

It will be September.
We will note another summer gone.
The ash will shimmer its small change,
the ground be covered with crab apples
that six months past were blossoms
white and pink in new light.
Over us swallows stroke and sail
the updrafts of a few, last perfect days.
The years will have peeled us
thin as ash, white as apple blossoms.

We come from tending the rows,
find ourselves walking on
windfall peaches in the north yard.
They will be all over the ground,
gold-dusted, giving softly

under the balls of our feet,
size of apricots, no good for eating,
but the smell will be
delicious.

Equinox

Day is already slipping from the porch,
but beyond, the retreating sun still hangs
like a curtain in the forest.
A few, slim circles of trees
stand in shafts of light, as if
it were just morning there
in some vestibule of pines,
just midday amid the farther sweet gum,
and one might enter those woods
to step in and out of whatever
hour one would choose.

It is still light enough to read,
but I have put the thick book by,
content to wait out the onset
of evening. Out of the stillness
my husband starts up the mower
from the front of the house,
its rough blurt overriding all
but the occasional cries of children
down by the road.

Though this is my home,
it seems I should be gathering wood
for a fire to be built in a ring
of stones, with flint taken
from a tin, or with knots of paper
in parafin. A smell, as of old
earth and bark, comes up to me.
But there is nothing waiting for me,
nothing I need do, adrift
in the curious no-weather between
summer and fall. I have only
to sit here in the cedar-planked chair,
my coffee gone cold on its arm,

and look off into the understory
where late sun lies like scattered
gold at the bottom of grottoes,
single leaves coined in that
momentary brilliance that seems,
like the peak in some lives,
too dazzling for aftermath.

Children glint in the underbrush
bent to their private paths, far
from mower and porch alike.
I am not thinking of them,
I am not thinking of love,
no longer do I ask about change.
Instead I am thinking, this
is what I wanted, this is
what I asked for,
the quiet, the stillness,
to be here quite still and alone,
to follow the light as it trails
back and back, into the mere
imagination of woodland,
where my eyes finally lose track.
But not entirely quiet—
there is always
the crick and snap of things
that drop straight or drift
to the ground, somewhere, something
is always making its way down,
and yet how fixed,
how motionless
the whole remains.